PLANET ASPERGER

AROUND THE SYNDROME IN 88 QUESTIONS

CÉDRIC H. ROSERENS

TABLE OF CONTENTS

PROVERB

"If you know an autist,
you know an autist."

— *autistic proverb*

FOREWORD

This little introductory guide to Asperger's syndrome is the one I wish I had in my hands 20 or 30 years ago. I was diagnosed with Asperger's syndrome at the age of 45. It was like someone lit up a candle in my brain. Everything became crystal clear. Everything finally made sense.

Right after the diagnosis, the Greek and Roman adages "Know thyself" and "Knowledge is power" came to my mind, as well as hundreds of questions. This little book gives you my answers to 88 of them. 88, like the number of constellations in the night sky. 88, like the number of keys on a piano. The answers are the result of my personal experience and of my post-diagnosis readings. This guide is intentionally basic. For a more academic view, see the bibliographical references.

Have a nice journey in an aspie brain!

Cédric H. Roserens

Thessaloniki (Greece)

September 2020

info@chroserens.com

PROLOGUE

It was a chilly December-2019 evening in Budapest. I had a seat in the front row of the first screening of Star Wars IX. When I heard the line "Never be afraid of who you are..." that was it. I knew it. I am an Asperger. *Ich bin ein Asperger.*

This is an urban legend.

The reality is a little bit more complicated.

The diagnosis was made after I went through divorce, post-traumatic stress, depression, anxiety, and persistent social anxiety. It was first made via a series of online tests. Then via a consultation with a specialized psychologist in Reykjavík.

QUESTION 1

WHAT IS A SYNDROME?

A syndrome is a collection of symptoms.

QUESTION 2

WHAT ARE THE MAIN SYMPTOMS OF ASPERGER'S SYNDROME?

On the plus side:
honesty, loyalty, reliability.

On the minus side: difficulties with social interactions, lack of some motor skills, repetitive behaviours.

On the neutral side: restricted interests and sensory perception.

These symptoms are detailed later in the book.

QUESTION 3

WHAT IS THE
AUTISM SPECTRUM?

Add to the aforementioned symptoms of Asperger's syndrome both speech and learning difficulties, and you get what is called the autism spectrum, or more commonly autism.

Each symptom can be: strong, medium, weak, or non-existent, depending on the individual we are talking about.

Consequently: each autistic person is a unique, distinct individual, with his own palette of symptoms, strengths, and weaknesses.

QUESTION 4

WHAT IS AN ASPIE?

An aspie is a person diagnosed with Asperger's syndrome.

Asperger's syndrome is also known as Asperger's.

QUESTION 5

WHAT IS THE DIFFERENCE BETWEEN AN AUTIST AND AN ASPIE?

An aspie is autistic. An autist is not necessarily an aspie.

An aspie is an autist without speech or learning difficulties.

Aspie + speech difficulties + learning difficulties = autist.

Autist without speech or learning difficulties = aspie.

Got it?

QUESTION 6

WHAT IS THE DIFFERENCE
BETWEEN ASPERGER'S
AND ASPIE?

None.

QUESTION 7

WHAT DOES IT HAVE TO DO WITH ASPARAGUS?

Nothing.

QUESTION 8

WHO IS HANS ASPERGER?

Asperger's syndrome owes its name to the Austrian psychologist Johann "Hans" Friedrich Karl Asperger (1906-1980), who was the first to identify a group of unusual children, the aspies.

QUESTION 9

WHAT DOES NEUROTYPICAL MEAN?

Non-autistic.

QUESTION 10

HOW DO YOU BECOME ASPIE?

You are born aspie.

QUESTION 11

HOW LONG DO YOU STAY ASPIE?

All your life.

QUESTION 12

AT WHAT AGE IS
AN ASPIE SPOTTED?

Aspies can be spotted early in their
childhood or late in their adulthood,
or not at all because they are good
at going unnoticed.

QUESTION 13

WHAT SYMPTOMS ARE SPOTTED DURING CHILDHOOD?

Repetitive behaviours (alignment of toys, compulsive movements of the hands or fingers, etc.) and restricted interests (passion for dinosaurs but no interest in the rest of the animals, for example).

QUESTION 14

WHAT SYMPTOMS ARE SPOTTED DURING ADOLESCENCE?

Social interaction difficulty is a visible sign during adolescence, notably in the case of bullying, one of the most painful wounds in the life of an aspie. Any non-standard person is indeed a potential victim of bullying during adolescence.

Aspies are no exception.

QUESTION 15

DO SYMPTOMS DISAPPEAR DURING ADULTHOOD?

Some symptoms go away over the years, others do not. Some decrease or disappear depending on the ability of the aspie to adapt to the neurotypical world

Other symptoms have no interest in disappearing because they are strengths rather than weaknesses.

QUESTION 16

CAN YOU SPEND ALL YOUR LIFE NOT KNOWING YOU ARE AN ASPIE?

Yes, you can.

Because of the absence of speech and learning difficulties, and of their great adaptability, aspies can go unnoticed for a large part of their life. This explains why they are sometimes nicknamed the invisible autists.

QUESTION 17

ARE ASPIES STRONG WITH THE FORCE?

If being an aspie can appear as a handicap in a world formatted for neurotypical people, aspies do not lack assets in their game, notably honesty, loyalty, and reliability.

So, yes, the Force is strong with the aspies, even if they have to live with some dark sides.

QUESTION 18

TOO HONEST TO BE TRUE?

The flip side of the honest aspies is that they may be too honest. They will say frankly what they think without measuring the consequences and while possibly hurting their interlocutors.

QUESTION 19

DO ASPIES HAVE
ANY PREJUDICE?

Little.

Well below the neurotypical average.

QUESTION 20

IS THE DEVIL REALLY
IN THE DETAILS?

Aspies perceive the details better than the whole. They can be particularly good at this game, spotting miles away a spelling error or a broken alignment where ordinary people will miss it
or will not see anything special.

QUESTION 21

ALWAYS ON TIME, THE ASPIE IS?

As reliable as a Swiss watch.

QUESTION 22

IS PLANNING IMPORTANT FOR AN ASPIE?

The more organized, the more predictable.

And aspies like the predictable.

QUESTION 23

PLANNING OR OVER-PLANNING?

Planning reassures the aspies. Less uncertainty. Less anxiety.

To the point of over-planning, at the expense of flexibility, a quality that they often lack.

QUESTION 24

DO ASPIES COME FROM VULCAN?

The inhabitants of the planet Vulcan and their most prominent representative, Spock, are renowned for their keen sense of logic. Just like aspies.

If Vulcan existed, it could well have been the home planet of the aspies.

QUESTION 25

ARE ASPIES TOO RIGID?

Their excess of logic, planning,
and organization can turn them
into unmovable stones.

QUESTION 26

WHAT ARE THE MAIN WEAKNESSES OF AN ASPIE?

The main ones are social interactions, lack of some motor skills, naivety, anxiety, and hypersensitivity. They are described in the next questions.

QUESTION 27

DOES ISABELLE
HAVE BLUE EYES?

Do not ask an aspie. Eye contact is not his
cup of tea, so it may take years for an aspie
to realize that yes, Isabelle does indeed
have blue eyes (one of the few details that
the aspie may fail to notice).

QUESTION 28

DO ASPIES UNDERESTIMATE THEMSELVES?

The lack of self-esteem is also one of the weaknesses of the aspie. It results from the fact that the aspie neither manages to keep up with the neurotypical pace (everything is going too fast), nor obtains the same successes as his non-autistic peers.

QUESTION 29

IS NAIVETY THE ACHILLES' HEEL OF YOUNG ASPIES?

Yes. They innocently believe that everyone is nice. They quickly become disillusioned and learn to lose their innocence while separating the wheat from the chaff in those around them.

QUESTION 30

DO ASPIES HAVE FRIENDS?

Yes. Usually less than neurotypicals,
but long-lasting friendships.

QUESTION 31

SOCIAL ANXIETY, A CONSTANT AMONG ASPIES?

Absolutely. Aspies enjoy seeing their small circles of friends more than having to create new circles.

QUESTION 32

WHAT IS SOCIAL FATIGUE?

It is the accumulation of social interactions, which results in too high a mental load for the aspie brain.

QUESTION 33

WHY IS IT EXHAUSTING TO BE AN ASPIE?

By navigating a neurotypical society that is not calibrated for him, the aspie gets exhausted. His batteries drain with every conversation, at every meeting, at every social interaction. They have a lower capacity than those of neurotypicals.

QUESTION 34

WHY DO ASPIES
NEED SOLITUDE?

To be able to reload their batteries in peace, as long and as often as necessary, away from the neurotypical hubbub.

QUESTION 35

ARE ANXIETY AND DEPRESSION THE DEVILS OF THE ASPIE WORLD?

Anxiety is part of aspies' DNA.

Depression is also common there.

Living in a neurotypical world, with its high social standards and expectations, is not always easy for the aspies. It is a source of daily anxiety and of possible depression.

QUESTION 36

WHAT ABOUT SUICIDES?

The suicide rate among people on the autism spectrum is 7 to 10 times higher than that of neurotypicals, according to some studies. Other studies are underway to confirm (or contradict) these results.

The causes of this rate difference are also being analysed. Consequence of common anxiety and depression?
Or from constantly feeling like a stranger in a neurotypical world?
Accumulation of social fatigue?
To be confirmed/contradicted…

QUESTION 37

WHAT ABOUT
LIFE EXPECTANCY?

Autistic people live on average fifteen years less than neurotypicals and aspies ten years less. Other studies are underway to confirm (or contradict) these figures.

Is this related to the higher suicide rate, the higher prevalence of anxiety and depression, or due to a weakened immune system? To be confirmed/contradicted…

QUESTION 38

DO ASPIES GET DOUBLE MEANINGS AND SARCASM?

The aspies say what they think, without giving it a second thought. The divergence of meaning between what is said and what is implied is not natural to them, whether it is sarcasm or irony. That said, they learn over time.

QUESTION 39

HOW DO ASPIES COPE WITH THE ART OF CONVERSATION?

When to speak? When to interrupt? When to listen without interrupting? The art of conversation is a difficult one for an aspie to grasp, especially if the interlocutors are numerous and noisy.

QUESTION 40

DO ASPIES

LACK EMPATHY?

No. They do not always know how to express it.

QUESTION 41

DO ASPIES PRACTICE IRISH GOODBYES?

Yes. If aspies are bored or drowned in the hubbub of a group of neurotypicals, they will use the pretext of going to the toilet to slip away or will evaporate through an open window without anyone noticing.

QUESTION 42

ARE ASPIES

FASHION VICTIMS?

Clothing and haircuts are not the main concerns of aspies, unless fashion is one of their restricted interests, or if it is Carnival.

QUESTION 43

WHAT ABOUT RESTRICTED INTERESTS?

They are the hallmark of autistic people and aspies.

Restricted interests can go unnoticed if they are common among neurotypicals (football, stamp collecting, chess)
but can be easily spotted if they are unusual (vexillology, hornuss, dinosaurs).

QUESTION 44

ARE ASPIES HYPERSENSITIVE?

The five senses of an aspie can be significantly more developed than those of a typical neurotypical. Each aspie having a different profile, it is one, two, three, four or five senses, or even six, which are potentially concerned, with varying intensity. This can be an advantage or a disadvantage, depending on the case.

Examples in the next five questions...

QUESTION 45

OH, ASPIE, WHY DO YOU HAVE SUCH BIG EARS?

To hear you better,
dear smartphone notification.

A simple smartphone notification
may startle the aspie.

QUESTION 46

OH, ASPIE, WHY DO YOU HAVE SUCH BIG EYES?

To observe you better,
dear blinking Christmas decoration.

*A blinking Christmas decoration can make
the aspie feel like in a nightclub in Ibiza.*

QUESTION 47

OH, ASPIE, WHY DO YOU HAVE SUCH BIG HANDS?

To touch you better,
dear trendy jeans.

*The aspie can struggle to find clothes
with a texture that suits him.*

QUESTION 48

OH, ASPIE, WHY DO YOU HAVE SUCH A BIG MOUTH?

To savour you better,
dear ten-spice tagine.

Aspies can better appreciate
some aromatic subtleties than neurotypicals.

QUESTION 49

OH, ASPIE, WHY DO YOU HAVE SUCH A BIG NOSE?

To smell you better,
dear fragrance of a distant bakery.

*Aspies can perceive from a long distance
what a neurotypical will only perceive
at a close range.*

QUESTION 50

WHAT IS THE DEAL WITH COORDINATION?

Aspies may have difficulty coordinating the movements of their arms and legs (psychomotor disorder).

Gymnastic exercises, skating, swimming, dancing, etc., can represent challenges hard to meet, even with extensive training.

QUESTION 51

WHAT CAUSES SENSORY OVERLOAD?

Some common everyday situations,
such as the fateful moment of the
checkout at the supermarket.
The aspie brain struggles to keep up
because there is too much going on at the
same time (social interaction, payment,
arranging items in the bag, pressure from
the waiting customers in the queue).
No wonder aspies may prefer
to shop online.

QUESTION 52

WHAT ABOUT DRIVING?

Driving is a difficult mission for an aspie. Too many elements to manage at the same time: looking at the front, looking at the sides, looking at the back, rain, the heating system, the audio system, speed, the tank level, braking, accelerating, etc.
If the car is not automatic and the aspie has coordination issues (arms and legs), the mission becomes impossible.

QUESTION 53

TAURINE, ADRENALINE, CAFFEINE?

The aspie says: no thanks.

Or in small quantities.

Life is already going fast enough.

QUESTION 54

DO ASPIES HAVE REPETITIVE BEHAVIOURS?

Yes, they do.

QUESTION 55

DO ASPIES HAVE REPETITIVE BEHAVIOURS?

Yes, they do.

QUESTION 56

DO ASPIES HAVE REPETITIVE BEHAVIOURS?

Yes, they do.

QUESTION 57

WHY THESE REPETITIVE BEHAVIOURS?

Also called fidgeting, repetitive behaviours calm and reassure aspies like other autistic people. Examples: spinning a pen in the hand, making hair curls with fingers, repeating a mantra, hitting the ball thirty-three times on the ground before serving in tennis, etc. Unlike tics and OCD (obsessive-compulsive disorder), repetitive behaviours are not necessarily involuntary.

QUESTION 58

DO ASPIES LIKE
TO COLLECT THINGS?

Often. Because they like classification
and repetitive behaviours. From stamps to
baseball cards, butterflies, sea or military
shells, autographs, cheese or wine labels,
beer capsules, there is something for all
tastes and all colours on the autism
spectrum, as well as outside of it...

QUESTION 59

DO ASPIES
FEAR CHANGES?

In spite of all their goodwill to adapt to the neurotypical world, the need for routine prevails for the aspies, thus is any change or unforeseen event unwelcome at best.

QUESTION 60

WHAT ABOUT THE PROFESSIONAL LIFE OF AN ASPIE?

Clear instructions, calm environment,
daily routine, taking into account
his sensory specificities, and the aspie
will feel at ease in the office.

Silicon Valley is an example to follow in the
integration of aspies, which play there the role of
fuel for innovation, with some success, to say the
least. The Danes of *Specialisterne* aim to provide
employment for one million autistic people.
The German *SAP* and the Swiss-German *Asperger
Informatik* are also on the right wavelength by
betting on the potential of autistic people.
Even the Israeli military uses autistic intelligence
for sophisticated data analysis.

QUESTION 61

DO CLEAR INSTRUCTIONS MAKE THE ASPIE SHINE?

Clearly.

QUESTION 62

IS DAILY ROUTINE
AN ABSOLUTE NECESSITY
FOR AN ASPIE?

Absolutely.

QUESTION 63

ARE ASPIES MORE AT RISK FOR BURNOUT?

An aspie in the wrong place at work is a time bomb towards professional exhaustion (aka burnout).

QUESTION 64

SHOULD ASPIES REMAIN HIDDEN AT WORK?

It depends on the open-mindedness of their employers and co-workers.

QUESTION 65

DOES THE ASPIE LACK INITIATIVE?

The aspie performs his tasks perfectly if provided with clear rules, routines, or procedures.

But as soon as it is necessary to scratch further, out of frame, to go the extra mile, the aspie is no longer in his element.

QUESTION 66

WHAT ABOUT
TEAM SPIRIT?

The aspie can fit into a team,
preferably a small and stable one.

QUESTION 67

WHY IS OPEN SPACE LIKE HELL FOR AN ASPIE?

Because it promotes social interactions and constant hubbub, sworn enemies of the quiet aspie.

QUESTION 68

WHAT ABOUT
CORPORATE CAFETERIAS?

Chatter and hubbub being neither
his cup of tea or coffee, the aspie
will not spend much time in there.

QUESTION 69

AND CORPORATE AFTERWORK DRINKS?

Same consideration as for cafeterias, unless the aspie is very thirsty or has a special interest in beer, wine, or cocktails.

QUESTION 70

MUST WE SAVE
PRIVATE ASPIAN?

Yes. But do not try to make him a corporal
or a lieutenant. As much as the aspie is a
good soldier, the management of a team
and its interpersonal conflicts, often
irrational, are not a field he will
blossom in.

QUESTION 71

WHAT ABOUT THE SENTIMENTAL LIFE OF AN ASPIE?

The difficulty in spotting the signs coming from potential mates makes the sentimental life of an aspie look like an obstacle run, or the crossing of a desert, unless he finds a partner who is on the autism spectrum, on a non-neurotypical wavelength, or particularly open-minded.

QUESTION 72

WHAT ABOUT THE RELIGIOUS LIFE OF AN ASPIE?

Like a double-sided coin. The rational side of the aspie can make him opt for atheism, agnosticism, or humanism. The reassuring side of a rule-based religion that flags the path from life to death (and beyond) can also attract aspies.

QUESTION 73

WHAT ABOUT
THE POLITICAL LIFE
OF AN ASPIE?

Aspies do not know how to lie.
And talking to say nothing is a concept
unknown to them. Furthermore, they are
honest and tend to say out loud what they
think. Therefore, they have little chance of
a noticeable career in politics among
neurotypicals.

QUESTION 74

HOMEBODY
OR TRAVELLER?

Aspies feel abroad everywhere, even at home. The elsewhere is not more difficult for them to manage than the here, which makes them first-rate candidates for exotic journeys, since they will not feel less comfortable with the customs and traditions of elsewhere than with the customs and traditions of their motherland.

Some aspies have the opposite tendency, though, and prefer to stay in their usual environment and its routines, thus making perfect homebodies.

QUESTION 75

WHAT IS THE CAUSE
OF AUTISM?

Complex genetic factors are at the root of autism. Scientists (geneticists and neurobiologists) are discovering new genes linked to autism year after year. Piece by piece, they put together the puzzle of the mystery of the origins of autism.

The advancement of scientific research in genetics and neurobiology makes obsolete the hazardous conclusions issued by psychoanalysts in the past century and their unfortunate consequences (parents' guilt, sending autistic children to institutions).

QUESTION 76

DO ASPIES HAVE
A DIFFERENT BRAIN?

Some parts of the aspie brain have a significantly different volume from the equivalent parts of the neurotypical brain, especially the cerebellum. In addition, many connections differ. This causes the aspie brain to work differently.

These differences are an advantage or a disadvantage, depending on the situation.

QUESTION 77

CAN YOU GET AUTISM FROM A VACCINE?

The first visible signs of autism (speech and learning difficulties) appear at the same time as the administration of the first vaccines.

This is a coincidence.

There is no correlation.

QUESTION 78

HOW TO CURE AUTISM?

Is it really a disease to be
honest, loyal, and reliable?

Autism can be cured quite simply with
the same drugs as for homosexuality:
five tablets a day of open-mindedness
and a good daily dose of mutual respect.

These medicines are to be prescribed for
neurotypicals as well as for autistic people.

QUESTION 79

IS AUTISM NECESSARY?

Without autistic people and their
unconventional thinking, humans
would probably still be in a cave
chatting and chowing down on their
lifelong dish of the day: mammoth
tartare and forest berries. Until someone
manages to sharpen a flint, tame fire,
invent the wheel, and channel electricity.

To wipe out autism is to give up
on future Mozarts or Einsteins;
it is against neurodiversity.

QUESTION 80

WHAT IS NEURODIVERSITY?

It is a school of thought which favours neurological diversity, and therefore advocates the integration of autistic people and any other non-neurotypical people in an inclusive society that emphasizes their strengths. It is the equivalent of biodiversity on a plant and animal scale.

QUESTION 81

HOW ANCIENT IS AUTISM?

The first conclusions of geneticists
show that genes linked to autism
have been present in humans since
the dawn of time.

Autism is as old as the world
(and thus much older than
the invention of vaccines).

QUESTION 82

DO AUTISTS HAVE SUPERPOWERS?

It depends on the dice of genetics, and on the specific brain connections of some specific autistic people.

Autists with superpowers are therefore the exception, not the rule. A well-known example: Raymond Babbitt in *Rain Man* (instant counting of toothpicks, extraordinary mental arithmetic capacity, etc.).

QUESTION 83

ARE ALL ASPIES GENIUSES?

No. However,

numerous geniuses are aspies.

QUESTION 84

CAN YOU NAME A FEW?

Some artists and scientists, considered as geniuses in their fields, do exhibit autistic traits and can be included in the aspie community. Here are twelve of them: Emily Dickinson, Greta Thunberg, Marie Curie, Michelangelo, Wolfgang Amadeus Mozart, Hans Christian Andersen, Lewis Carroll, Charles Darwin, Henry Cavendish, Isaac Newton, Albert Einstein, and Steve Jobs.

QUESTION 85

WHAT PERCENTAGE OF THE POPULATION IS AUTISTIC?

At least 1% of the population, half of which is aspie (0.5%).

Some recent estimates even say 2% (autists) and 1% (aspies).

QUESTION 86

WHAT TO DO
TO MAKE THE WORLD
MORE ASPIE-FRIENDLY?

Increase the level of knowledge
about the autism spectrum
in the neurotypical population...

Invent a common language that serves as
a bridge between Autistan and Normalia,
like braille or sign language; emoticons
are perhaps the root of it...

Generalize the concept of specific opening
hours for autistic people in supermarkets

(without sound advertising, with
reduced lighting, without pressure
at the checkouts), as is the case
in New Zealand...

Popularize speed-dating experiences and
lessons in seduction for non-neurotypical
people, as is the case in Australia...

Promote silent discos...

Set up aspie-cafés and aspie-bars in which
calm and zen would reign to not need
aspie-rine once back home. The idea
of an inclusive bar has just emerged
in the French part of Switzerland
(aka Romandy)...

Etc.

QUESTION 87

HOW TO BE DIAGNOSED?

A pre-diagnosis is possible online, but it is not sufficient (*for details, see the postface*).

A full diagnosis by a psychologist (specialized in autism) is highly recommended to refine the preliminary online analysis.

QUESTION 88

POST DIAGNOSIS LUX?

After the diagnosis, the light?

Yes, everything lights up.

And life goes on,
taking better into account
one's own strengths and weaknesses.

EPILOGUE

Let me end with a quick zoom on my pre-diagnosis professional life...

In spite of my undiagnosed autism (Asperger's syndrome), my career has been quite a successful one in the field of IT. No matter what the mission was (user support, training, writing news, writing web content, writing exam questions, etc.), no matter what the context was (banking, watchmaking, service company, work-at-home, digital nomadism, etc.).

Only one big downside, though, my burnout of 2009. It came as the result of an exhaustion caused by two major changes which proved to be incompatible with my aspie DNA. Firstly, the transition from a small team in a small office to a large open space. Secondly, from a job judged on quality to the very same job judged on quantity. An avoidable burnout, if only I had known I was an aspie.

Now equipped with a brand-new rudder (the diagnosis), it will be much easier to navigate through the occasional storms of the professional life sea.

May this book allow a potential aspie to recognize him/herself and avoid burnout!

POSTFACE

Do you want to do a pre-diagnosis online?

Just ask your favourite search engine
to find the following four tests for you:

Aspie Quiz

Autistic Quotient (AQ)

RAADS-14 Screen (Ritvo Autism & Asperger Diagnostic Scale)

RMET (Reading the Mind in the Eyes Test).

BIBLIOGRAPHY

Attwood, Tony (2008). *The Complete Guide to Asperger's Syndrome*. London: Jessica Kingsley Publishers.

Attwood, Tony (2014) et alli. *Been There. Done That. Try This!: An Aspie's Guide to Life on Earth*. London: Jessica Kingsley Publishers.

Dachez, Julie et Mademoiselle Caroline (2016). *La Différence Invisible*. Paris: Delcourt.

Friedman, Matt (2012). *Dude, I'm An Aspie!: Thoughts and Illustrations on Living with Asperger's Syndrome*. Morrisville: Lulu.com.

Grandin, Temple (2014). *The Autistic Brain: Thinking Across the Spectrum*. Boston: Mariner Books.

Grinker, Roy Richard (2021). *Nobody's Normal: How Culture Created the Stigma of Mental Illness*. New York: W. W. Norton & Company

Horiot, Hugo (2018). *Autisme: j'accuse!*
Paris: L'Iconoclaste.

Pillet, Isabel (2014). *Odyssée en Pays Asperger*.
Saint-Gall: Autismusverlag.

Schovanec, Josef (2015). *Éloge du Voyage à l'Usage des Autistes et de ceux qui ne le sont pas assez*. Paris: Pocket.

Schovanec, Josef (2013). *Je suis à l'Est!*
Paris: Pocket.

Silberman, Steve (2016). *NeuroTribes: The Legacy of Autism and How to Think Smarter About People Who Think Differently*.
London: Atlantic Books.

Simone, Rudy (2010). *Asperger's on the Job: Must-Have Advice for People with Asperger's or High Functioning Autism and their Employers, Educators, and Advocates*. Arlington: Future Horizons.

ACKNOWLEDGEMENTS

Thank you to my family and to my friends for being my guides on this strange planet.

Thanks a lot to the many proofreaders who helped me improve this book:

Christina CUTTING

Corinne SAUGE

Françoise ZINGG

Gilles TACCHINI

Karim DI MATTEO

Laetitia DONQUE

Laurence ABBET

Nicolas SUMMERMATTER

ABOUT THE AUTHOR

Cédric Henri Roserens was born in Martigny, Valais, Switzerland, in 1974. Too late to be James Cook and explore the infinite waters of the Pacific Ocean. Too early to be James T. Kirk and explore the infinite paths of our Galaxy. In 1999, he earned a Master of Arts degree from the University of Lausanne in computer science and geography. His travel experiences are an inexhaustible source of inspiration for his books.

Author's Website:

CHROSERENS.COM

ALSO BY
C.H. ROSERENS

"EIGHTY-ONE STOPOVERS", POEMS, 2015

From Rome to Wadi Rum, North Cape to Cape Leeuwin, Andorra to Zanzibar, Ireland to Iceland, Ottawa to Tonga, Tokyo, Kyoto, Quito...

A poetic tribute to Earth with a hidden goal: to make you pack&go see the world for yourself.

"UNCLE GREG'S TREASURE", NOVEL, 2017

A Wishing Shelf Book Awards 2018 finalist. An epistolary adventure around the world. Jetlag guaranteed!

Forky's banking career is brutally interrupted on the eve of his 40th birthday, to go find a treasure that no bank could store.

"HAPPÍSLAND", SHORT STORY, 2015

A first shot of Iceland with an aftertaste of rotten shark. A small unpretentious introduction to Iceland's way of life, focusing on Reykjavík.

Swiss superspy Hans-Ueli Stauffacher is sent to Iceland for one full calendar year to understand why Icelandic people are happier than Swiss people.

"FANTASVISS", SHORT STORY, 2019

An alternative guide to Switzerland, with a pint of irony and a drop of causticity. A condensed introduction to the 26 cantons of the Confederation.

Superspy Sigmundur Sig Sigmundsson is sent to Switzerland for one month to learn why Swiss people are happier than Icelandic people.

"THE LAST AUTIST", SHORT STORY, 2021

A crucial journey to Macaronesia.

Diagnosed with Asperger's syndrome in his mid-forties, Cédric H. Roserens used writing as a therapy. The result: an aspie trilogy, an autistic triptych composed of the short dystopia *The Last Autist*, the miniguide *Planet Asperger*, and the fairy tale *The Autistic Prince*.

"THE AUTISTIC PRINCE", FAIRY TALE, 2021

A journey worth a thousand strudels.

Diagnosed with Asperger's syndrome in his mid-forties, Cédric H. Roserens used writing as a therapy. The result: an aspie trilogy, an autistic triptych composed of the short dystopia *The Last Autist*, the miniguide *Planet Asperger*, and the fairy tale *The Autistic Prince*.

BOOKSHOP

All about Cédric H. Roserens' books:

CHROSERENS.COM/BOOKSHOP

Also available in French:

"HUITANTE ESCALES", POÈMES, 2014

"HAPPÍSLAND", COURT RÉCIT, 2015

"LE TRÉSOR D'ONCLE GREG", ROMAN, 2017

"FANTASVISS", COURT RÉCIT, 2019

"LE DERNIER AUTISTE", NOUVELLE, 2021

"PLANÈTE ASPERGER", MINIGUIDE, 2021

"LE PRINCE AUTISTE", CONTE DE FÉES, 2021

Printed in Great Britain
by Amazon